CALIF

Lake
Tahoe

Sacramento

Napa

Berkeley
Oakland

San Francisco

Sierra Nevada

Yosemite
National Park

Palo Alto
San Jose

Kings Canyon
National Park

CALIFORNIA

Monterey

Sequoia
National Park

Big Sur

Death Valley

Mojave Desert

Base
Edwards

PACIFIC OCEAN

Santa Barbara

Ojai Valley

Malibu

Los Angeles

Long
Beach

NORTH CALIFORNIA

Eureka

Lassen Volcanic
National Park

Lake Tahoe

NEVADA

Joshua Tree
National Park

Palm
Springs

San Diego
Tijuana

GOLD
DISCOVERY
SITE

The Transamerica Pyramid is one of many landmarks in downtown San Francisco. Today, the city is a metropolis that blends modernity and tradition.

San Francisco, on the west coast of the United States, has attracted both American pioneers and foreign immigrants in search of the Californian dream of riches.

The Victorian face of America.

San Francisco

The island of Yerba Buena, located in the mouth of a cove, represented a strategic position on the west coast of North America. It was discovered by the Spaniards during the course of an overland expedition and became the base of Franciscan missionaries. It fell under the rule of Mexico and was later made over to the United States. Within a few months of the start of the Gold Rush, tens of thousands of people had descended on this little hamlet — and San Francisco was born.

San Francisco was originally little more than a small trading station.

Worried by the arrival of Russian trappers from Alaska, the Spanish government (which at that time ruled Mexico) decided to occupy California. In 1776, a handful of settlers, a few soldiers and a Franciscan friar founded a mission on the edge of the wide bay that lay to the

north of Monterey. With the influx of American pioneers, its population steadily grew. In July 1846, the little village was taken over by the United States and renamed San Francisco.

At the beginning of the 18th century, Spanish settlers began to inhabit California. From the Mexican border, Franciscan missionaries, under the leadership of Father Junípero Serra, established a total of 21 missions on the unknown lands of Northern California. Each were linked by El Camino Real, the 'Royal Way'.

San Francisco Bay is frequently shrouded in mist and thus lost from view. It was discovered not from the sea, but by a Spanish overland expedition.

In 1850, San Francisco was just a village at the foot of the mountains.

Most of the ships carrying adventurers to San Francisco never made the return voyage. Grabbed by gold fever, the crews abandoned their ships in order to seek their fortune.

The rush to San Francisco...

Until the beginning of 1848, San Francisco amassed its modest wealth chiefly by provisioning the small number of ships that put into port on the West Coast. Its inhabitants numbered scarcely more than 100. A discovery, however, was about to transform this small trading station for ever: to the north-west, in the direction of Sacramento, the American River was found to carry gold dust. As a result, everyone grabbed a sieve, a shovel and a firearm, deserting hearth and home to head for El Dorado. The news that gold was to be found spread like

After the Gold Rush, San Francisco expanded further as waves of immigrants arrived.

...and untold wealth

wildfire and soon it had reached other countries. From then on, San Francisco became a magnet for every pan-handler bent on trying his luck. People arrived from all over the world, mostly by boat, from as far afield as Europe and China. Within a few months, the village of San Francisco had become a chaotic campsite inhabited by more than 50,000 prospectors.

Those who made their way to California by an overland route undertook a long and perilous journey.

On the Barbary Coast, where lawlessness ruled, bandits would lie in wait for newcomers, welcoming them with offers of alcohol and cabaret shows.

For a long time, Chinatown was a den of iniquity, where prostitution, opium dens and gambling houses thrived alongside Chinese laundries.

The opening of the transcontinental railway in 1869 made it possible to cross the United States from east to west in just six days.

Dim sum...in downtown San Francisco.

Shopkeepers grew rich and soon San Francisco's geographical isolation became a hindrance to its development. In 1862, Congress approved a budget for the construction of a transcontinental railway and Central Pacific, the company charged with building the line from Oakland, took on thousands of Chinese labourers. When the project was completed in 1869, many of these unemployed immigrants headed for San Francisco.

The Chinese labourers contracted by Central Pacific worked under appalling conditions. By contrast, the new railway made the fortune of the Big Four, the four men at the head of Central Pacific.

Chinatown rubs shoulders with the financial district of San Francisco, offering some surprising contrasts.

Whilst the cable car made the hills more accessible, it also led to a rise in land prices.

A unique mode of transport

When they were first installed, cable cars sometimes went out of control. With no dead man's handle, all the driver could do was desperately sound the bell to warn pedestrians and other vehicles! The cable car could only be stopped by cutting the power to the entire line.

As the city grew, public transport became a problem. The grid pattern typical of American city planning was ill-suited to the uneven terrain of the 42 hills. In 1873, a Scottish immigrant came up with a solution to the problem, basing his ideas on the wagons used in English mines. He devised a system of tramways with cable cars capable of climbing even the steepest hill.

In 1964, by which time cars had already become the kings of the road, San Francisco's cable car network was declared a national monument.

The San Francisco earthquake was front-page news throughout the world.

San Francisco was reduced to rubble within a few hours.

A fault beneath the city

On April 18, 1906, a huge earthquake almost completely destroyed San Francisco. Apart from the buildings destroyed by the earthquake itself, gas mains were ruptured, leading to raging fires that only added to the crisis. By the time the inferno was finally brought under control by a providential downpour, some 3000 people were dead and 250,000 had been made homeless.

The anniversary of the San Francisco earthquake is a time when Americans remember the bravery with which the city's firemen tackled the enormous fires that raged in the city.

A disastrous decision

On April 18, 1906, the San Francisco emergency services soon found themselves overwhelmed by the fires sweeping through the city following the earthquake. The water mains had been damaged which meant that the fire brigade were deprived of their only means of putting out the fires. To make matters worse, rubble, flames and smoke prevented any effective coordination. As panic and disorder reigned, General Funston invoked martial law and took control of the emergency services. He gave orders to blow up several blocks of flats so as to stop the fires from spreading. Unfortunately, this made them burn even more fiercely. In the end, it was thanks to the rain that the fires were finally brought under control.

The Coit Memorial Tower was erected on Telegraph Hill in 1933. It was built with funds provided by Lillie Hitchcock Coit, nicknamed 'Firebell Lillie', a rich and eccentric heiress who held a special place in her heart for the firemen of San Francisco.

The city in ruins....

On April 21, 1906, San Francisco lay in ruins: more than 25,000 buildings had been reduced to ashes. While an international humanitarian aid effort was being organized, makeshift campsites were set up to house those people – half the population – who no longer had a roof over their heads. Already facing a shortage of water, they now had to contend with rats and disease. In these temporary camps, the spirit of mutual aid and solidarity that had enabled the population to survive the economic crises that followed the end of the Gold Rush was rekindled.

The Palace of Fine Arts was built in honour of the 1915 Pacific-Panama World Fair.

...rises like a phoenix

Thanks to the resolve of the population of San Francisco, and to the millions of dollars lent by banks on the East Coast of the United States, the city was swiftly rebuilt. In 1915, while World War I was raging in Europe, San Francisco was ready to host the Pacific-Panama World Fair, organized to mark the opening of the canal that flowed between North and South America.

San Francisco's colourfully painted houses, built in the English Victorian style, date from between 1860 and 1900. With their wooden frames, they survived the earthquake relatively well, although some were destroyed by the fire. Today, they are beautifully maintained by their owners.

High-rise buildings stand as a symbol of San Francisco's economic prosperity.

From gold-digging...

After the heady days of the Gold Rush, the city's Italian immigrants turned to fishing for their livelihood.

Wells Fargo's famous black and red stagecoaches recall the pioneering days of the Wild West.

If San Francisco allowed a small number of gold-diggers to make their fortune, credit for launching the city on the road to long-term success must go to its business community. From 1850 onwards, the service industry grew more and more rapidly. This was a city in a state of perpetual development where anything was possible since everything had still to be invented. The New

The Financial District forms the centre of San Francisco's economic activity. It bristles with skyscrapers that run the gamut of architectural styles, from the most traditional to the ultra-modern.

...to economic prosperity

York bankers of the Wells Fargo company opened a high-speed transport service from San Francisco that supplied the miners and brought gold pouring into their own coffers. Later, Amadeo Giannini opened a bank in a saloon and accepted one-dollar deposits made by small savers from the Italian community. Little did he know that his small business would eventually become the all-powerful Bank of America. After a successful investment in industry, San Francisco, as pioneering as ever, turned its attention to the Pacific Rim, and began to trade prosperously with Asian countries.

Levi Strauss Jeans & Co.

Levi Strauss was born in Bavaria in 1829 and at the age of 18 emigrated to the United States with his mother and two sisters. In New York, he joined the family business, a textile company established by his two stepbrothers. In 1853, at the age of 24, shortly after he had been granted American citizenship, he moved to San Francisco where he opened a small cotton-cloth and canvas business. Such was the demand for this heavyweight material, for the covers of wagons and for tents, that the business thrived. The young Levi Strauss then hit on the idea of using the offcuts to make work trousers for the local miners. Initially the cloth was brown. When supplies ran out, he switched to cloth from Nîmes, in the south of France, which was just as hard-wearing but dyed blue: denim jeans hit the world.

San Franciscans consider Lombard Street, lined with colourful flowerbeds, to be the most winding street in the world.

San Francisco, once home to the beatniks and the hippies, is shaped by a unique culture that espouses freedom of expression and beliefs.

The elegance of painted houses.

The spirit of Frisco

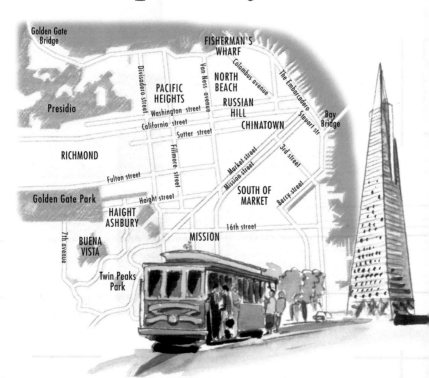

Golden Gate Bridge

FISHERMAN'S WHARF

Columbus avenue

The Embarcadero

Divisadero street

Van Ness avenue

NORTH BEACH

PACIFIC HEIGHTS

RUSSIAN HILL

Presidio

Washington street

Steuart str

Bay Bridge

California street

CHINATOWN

Sutter street

RICHMOND

Fillmore street

Market street

3rd street

Mission street

Fulton street

Golden Gate Park

Haight street

SOUTH OF MARKET

Berry street

HAIGHT ASHBURY

16th street

BUENA VISTA

MISSION

7th avenue

Twin Peaks Park

Jack Kerouac was born in Massachusetts and travelled all over the United States between 1942 and 1952. The novel that he wrote as the result of his experiences was On the Road *(1957). When it finally found a publisher, the book became the first best-seller of the Beat Generation. Beat culture was born with* Howl, *an anthology of poems by the New Yorker, Allen Ginsberg. At a party one evening in San Francisco in October 1955, Ginsberg gave a poetry reading, marking the rhythm of the words with his body. When the anthology was published a year later, the young publisher Lawrence Ferlinghetti faced prosecution for obscenity. Widely publicized, the case brought Beat culture to public attention.*

City Lights, founded by Ferlinghetti.

THE POCKET POETS SERIES

HOWL

AND OTHER POEMS

ALLEN GINSBERG

Introduction by

William Carlos Williams

NUMBER FOUR

In the 1950s, a new generation of Americans grew hungry for novelty and excitement, and a small group of alternative New York poets became their figurehead. The voyage of discovery made by Jack Kerouac and Allen Ginsberg began in the jazz clubs of New York and continued along the road that led to San Francisco, where they lived a bohemian existence in the immigrant quarter of North Beach.

In its heyday, the Vesuvio was a favourite haunt of the Beat Generation.

The Beat Generation

Their poetry was inspired by jazz, whilst drugs assisted them in their quest to give free rein to all the senses. In November 1959, *Life* magazine ran a feature on these 'rebels' and suddenly beatnik culture seemed to have taken over the United States. The term 'beatnik' – coined for those long-haired, barefooted adolescents who dreamed of a life without constraints, filled with jazz, travel and drugs – was regarded as an insult by the founder members, but the publicity brought them and San Francisco to the attention of the world's youth.

San Francisco's Italian quarter stretches from North Beach to Fisherman's Wharf. The Genoese and Sicilian immigrants have given the district a distinctly Mediterranean feel which was popular with the beatniks.

Champions of love, peace and happiness, the hippies invented psychedelic art, inspired by the imaginary shapes and colours conjured up by hallucinogenic drugs.

Flower power on the streets of San Francisco.

Make love not war

By the late 1950s, the Beat movement was no longer in the ascendant and in the 1960s, the banner of social change and artistic renewal was taken up by the hippies. Communities of students and artists grew up around Haight Street and Ashbury Street. The summer of 1967 became known as the Summer of Love and of LSD. Half a million young people flocked to San Francisco. The movement was short-lived but it was spread throughout the world by the music of Californian rock bands such as Jefferson Airplane and The Grateful Dead.

Many people are still highly nostalgic for the 1960s, from non-violence and karma to pirate radio stations that played rock all day long and bizarre works of art.

The church of Mission Dolores was founded by the Spaniards in 1776.

Mission and Castro

Mission District was one of the first areas of San Francisco to be settled by Hispanics. In the 1970s, with the influx of refugees fleeing the dictatorial regimes of South America, history seemed to be repeating itself. It is a district that still buzzes with revolutionary fervour and where the streets come alive with wall paintings – a host of murals expressing left-wing ideals.

For Latin American muralists, every wall painting is an opportunity to draw attention to the needs of the Hispanic community. This mode of artistic expression first appeared in San Francisco in the 1930s when Mexican artists were forced to flee the civil war in their country.

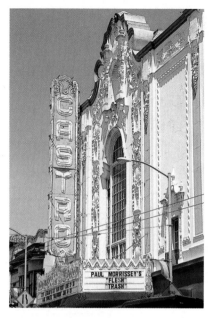

The façade of the Castro Theater.

Gays and lesbians, transvestites and transexuals – all shades of sexuality find social acceptance in San Francisco.

Castro is the gay district of San Francisco. Decked out with rainbow flags, it is as colourful as Mission District. The gay community was established in this historic quarter in the 1970s when homosexual soldiers expelled from the army during the Vietnam War chose to remain in their port of disembarkation rather than return to their families. With sexual liberation, the gay community now faces a new challenge: that of AIDS.

Gay Pride, at the end of June, is marked with a parade that winds through the streets of Castro. The out-rageous sights are only matched by those at an adult version of Halloween, at the end of October.

Many of the Victorian houses in Castro have been con-verted into shops selling all manner of unusual merchandise.

On its journey across the Atlantic and the American continent, the French game of boules *has been transformed into 'lawn bowling' (crown green bowling).*

The good life

The population of San Francisco is not, however, made up entirely of ethnic and cultural minorities. Like all other major American cities, San Francisco has not only endless suburbs

Here, as everywhere else in the United States, ball games, in the form of American football, basketball and baseball, are hugely popular.

but also an American football team (the Forty-Niners) and a baseball team (the famous San Francisco Giants). The parks are daily filled with dozens of joggers. This is also a typically Californian city

San Franciscans take a responsible attitude to the natural environment that surrounds them. These sea lions bask undisturbed on the walkways in the harbour.

San Francisco has welcomed many immigrants and is today a thoroughly cosmopolitan city.

Modern skyscrapers form a backdrop to one of the city's historic districts.

which has the great outdoors right on its doorstep. The Pacific Ocean, with its gentle winds, is a paradise for yachting enthusiasts, surfers and kite-flyers, and for hikers and ramblers, extensive parkland is also within easy reach. Unlike other large American cities, the centre of town is not completely overrun by commercial skyscrapers. The city's uneven terrain has been an antidote to the uniform regularity of the traditional grid-pattern of streets, giving it more of a European flavour. It is, however, the tolerance and cosmopolitan nature of San Francisco that give it its unique character.

The tiny Japanese Tea Garden, created at the end of the 19th century, is one of the most attractive features of Golden Gate Park. In the Japanese Tea House, tea is served by waitresses in kimonos.

Golden Gate Bridge, 220 feet (67 metres) long, spans Golden Gate, the strait at the entrance to San Francisco Bay through which ocean-going cargo ships sail.

Golden Gate Bridge stands as a symbol of success and as a gateway to the American Dream and the riches of the American West.

Crossing the American West.

San Francisco Bay

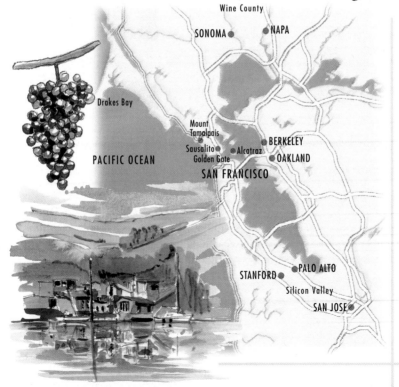

Wine County

SONOMA ● ● NAPA

Drakes Bay

Mount Tamalpais

Sausalito ● ● Alcatraz ● BERKELEY
Golden Gate ● OAKLAND

PACIFIC OCEAN

SAN FRANCISCO

PALO ALTO ●
STANFORD ● ●
Silicon Valley
SAN JOSE ●

Golden Gate Bridge, spanning almost 2 miles (3 km), is one of the longest in the world.

Scarlet steel piles, 745 feet (227 metres) tall, tower over San Francisco Bay. They are anchored in gigantic blocks of concrete capable of withstanding tides of up to 60 miles (100 kilometres) per hour.

San Francisco, set at the end of a rocky peninsula, is surrounded on three sides by water. A physical link with Marin County, on the opposite side of the Golden Gate, was obviously desirable. Plans for the construction of a bridge were first put forward at the beginning of the 20th century. The project was going to be challenge: the bridge had to withstand both the force of wind and tides and relatively frequent earth tremors. In the middle of the Great Depression, Joseph B. Strauss persuaded financiers to back his project. Charles E. Ellis was put in charge of draughting the plans and overcoming the many technical problems.

Golden Gate Bridge took five years to build. When it opened in 1937, it was hailed as an unrivalled technical achievement.

Before the Golden Gate Bridge was completed in 1937, tradegy struck when a platform collapsed, killing nine people.

Joseph B. Strauss also dreamed of building a bridge that would link North America with Russia at the Bering Strait.

The two cables that support the roadway are over 3 feet (1 m) thick. They consist of many strands of steel which together measure some 8000 miles (130,000 km).

A Herculean project

Thirty five million dollars, 1,765,750 cubic feet (500,000 cubic metres) of concrete and one million tonnes of steel were needed to build the Golden Gate Bridge which was officially opened in April 1937. Its elegant outline has come to stand as a symbol of San Francisco Bay, recognized throughout the world. One final statistic: no fewer than 40 million vehicles cross this imposing structure each year.

Even Al Capone, the notorious Chicago gangster, could not escape from Alcatraz.

The ghosts of Alcatraz

The island of Alcatraz ('Pelican Island' in Spanish) is a natural fortress. With an ideal strategic position at the mouth of the bay, it was used as a military stronghold from the mid-19th century. In 1907, the small fort on the island was converted into a military prison. In 1934, it became a federal penitentiary where the most dangerous criminals in the United States served their time. Notorious for its severe regime, its grim quasi-monastic cells and the tragic celebrity of its inmates, Alcatraz became known as the island from which no one escaped.

The lethal currents that swirl around Alcatraz make landing on the island, let alone escaping from it, virtually impossible. Only by using the landing stage can people set foot on the island without risking their lives.

Houseboats are an integral part of the urban landscape of San Francisco Bay.

Sausalito and the North

When the pontoons of the former military ship-yard at Sausalito fell into disuse, they were taken over by homeless people. With remarkable ingenuity and resourcefulness, they managed to build a village of houseboats.

In Sausalito, once a centre for whaling, luxury yachts grace the harbour.

At the dawn of the 20th century, a few wealthy San Franciscans, weary of the frenetic pace of urban life, made the move to the other side of the Golden Gate, settling near the whaling port of Sausalito. As maritime trade developed around the bay, so drinking dens, gambling joints and brothels followed, frequented by large numbers of sailors. Prohibition, bringing in its wake an army of

Strange homes made from bric-a-brac.

Sir Francis Drake, who discovered what is now called Drake's Bay (to the north of Sausalito), was one of the first explorers to land on the coast of California.

Mount Tamalpais, a favourite spot with hikers, is situated on the northern side of San Francisco Bay. On a clear day, it commands a magnificent view over the city.

bootleggers, put paid to the quiet respectability of this little community. During the war with Japan, Sausalito became a shipbuilding base for the US Navy, providing employment for the local population. However, after the closure of the naval dockyards at the end of World War II, old industrial sites were either turned into parks or left derelict. Today, Sausalito is once again home to the well-heeled middle classes.

Wooden houses, typical of northern California, cling to the steep hills of Sausalito.

Californian 'chateaux' produce wine to rival that of their European counterparts.

Sonoma and Napa...

The best Californian wines are produced in the Sonoma and Napa valleys, which stretch away to the north of San Francisco Bay. Sonoma has a historic centre, with picturesque buildings in the Spanish style. A flag emblazoned with a grizzly bear (once the flag of the short-lived Republic of California) flutters above Sonoma Plaza. This flag was hoisted in 1846 when American settlers imprisoned the Mexican governor of Sonoma and proclaimed their independence. It is now the official flag of the state of California. By the mid-

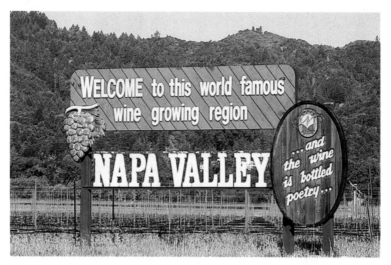

Californian vineyards grow such grapes as Cabernet, Chardonnay, Merlot and Pinot.

...the vineyards of California

19th century, California was already producing communion wine for the missions. However, it was Count Haraszthy, an aristocratic pioneer from Hungary with a passion for wine, who transformed California into a wine-growing region of international renown. By introducing major European varieties of grape to the area, he was able to improve the quality of locally grown wines. Prohibition interrupted the development of the Wine County, but today the 300 growers in both valleys still produce fine vintages.

Some wines from the Sonoma and Napa valleys are every bit as good as the best that France, Germany, Italy and Spain have to offer.

The University of California at Berkeley has always been a hotbed of student protest. It is a place where new and radical ideas are positively encouraged.

At Berkeley, the sit-ins that once took place on Sproul Plaza have today given way to the 'politically correct' movement that has swept America.

Sit-ins and demonstrations

The University of California at Berkeley was founded in 1868 and came to be regarded as the 'Athens of the West'. Berkeley came to prominence in the 1960s when, at a time when freedom of speech topped the agenda, students demanded the right of freedom of political expression on the campus. They also spoke out against racial discrimination, the death penalty and demonstrated against the Vietnam War. In more recent years, students have turned their attention to the United States' involvement in nuclear proliferation.

Some 30,000 students attend the University of California at Berkeley. The university is particularly strong in the field of humanities and social sciences. Over a dozen of its alumni have been Nobel Prize winners.

Racial segregation was once a part of daily life in Oakland.

An African-American district

Since its opening in 1936, Bay Bridge, linking San Francisco with Oakland, has been a convenient thoroughfare for San Franciscan workers travelling to the factories of Oakland by car.

Bay Bridge is a steel structure consisting of two superimposed roadways.

Oakland is a bustling metropolitan area that came into its own when it became a terminus for the transcontinental railway. It developed further with the increase in industrial and commercial activity around San Francisco Bay. As an industrial centre, it soon overtook San Francisco, and the opening of the bridge linking the two towns assured Oakland's continued success. After World

Jack London, the enfant terrible of Oakland.

War II, a large number of Black people flocked to this industrial town and in the 1960s, tension began to mount. It was in Oakland's Black ghetto that the Black Panther Party was founded in 1966, urging Black people to arm themselves against rough treatment by the police. Its militant members pursued a radical programme of social and political action and in 1977 the town finally elected a Black mayor.

The African-American community in Oakland is the town's largest ethnic minority. Although widely known as a Black town, Oakland also embraces a number of other ethnic communities, including Chinese, Korean, Vietnamese, Mexican, Italian and Portuguese.

Silicon Valley is a unique embodiment of the American Dream of economic success.

Silicon Valley

Silicon Valley, located to the south of San Francisco Bay, between Palo Alto and San José, came into being due to the presence of researchers working at Stanford University and the pioneering spirit of a few specialists in electronics. The star players, Hewlett Packard, Apple, Xerox and Intel, each owe their fortunes to the silicon chip. Innovation, miniaturization and technological revolution are the secret of their success which, in little more than 30 years, has overtaken the world and created the United States' most lucrative industry.

In the mid-1970s, Steve Jobs and Stephen Wozniak, working in a garage, built one of the first microcomputers. The Apple I was launched in 1976 and Apple II in 1977. IBM followed with its PC in the early 1980s.

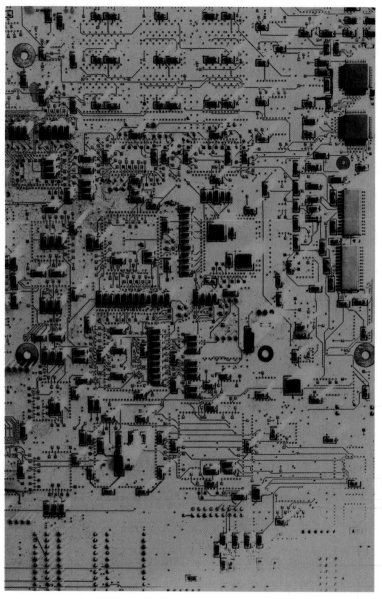

Silicon Valley, the heart of the computer industry, is named after the silicon microchip that made the miniaturization of electronic circuits possible.

Sacramento is the political capital of the State of California. The city's State Capitol, above, is the seat of the state's government.

Away from the busy cities of California, the countryside is rich in such natural wonders as Yosemite National Park and the Sierra Nevada.

Gold: the heritage of California.

Northern California

At the height of the Gold Rush, the mining town of Colombia was as important as Sacramento or even San Francisco.

In 1848, while building a sawmill north of Fort Sutter (the last trading post on the pioneer trail after the Sierra Nevada), James Marshall spotted a nugget of gold on the bed of the American River. He relayed the news to Johann Sutter, the owner of the land, who urged him not to tell a soul. The exciting news, however, did not remain a secret for long. It soon reached the ears of a San Franciscan journalist who, having craftily invested in

Gold washing was carried out in river beds where a pan was used to separate gold dust from the alluvial deposits. The lucky few even found nuggets, amassing small fortunes which, more often than not, were frittered away in the local saloons and gambling houses.

Mother Lode, the main gold deposit in the Sierra Nevada, was the destination of all the gold-diggers who headed from San Francisco to Fort Sutter (now part of Sacramento) in the hope of finding riches and making their fortunes.

Gold fever

a stock of digging tools, lost no time in spreading the rumour that in the depths of the Californian wilderness, gold was to be had by the shovelful. The affair mushroomed beyond his wildest dreams and by the next day, spades and picks were suddenly worth their weight in gold. The great Californian Gold Rush had begun. In the weeks that followed, people from all over the world came to try their luck in the foothills of the Sierra Nevada. The first prospectors to arrive throughout 1849 (subsequently known as the Forty-Niners) were rewarded with untold wealth. From

Johann Sutter's lost dream

In 1839, Johann Sutter left his native Switzerland to start a new life in California. He had the Utopian vision of establishing a New Helvetia on this virgin territory and purchased from the Mexican government more than 54,000 acres (20,000 hectares) of land. Sutter then cleared and developed his vast estate which, by 1848, was a self-contained private empire. That year, however, gold was discovered on his land and he could only stand by helplessly as tens of thousands of fortune-seekers invaded his property. Completely ruined, when in reality he was potentially the richest man in the world, he left the West Coast and put his case before Congress in Washington, but to no avail. He is thought to have died in Washington in 1880, in a state of penury.

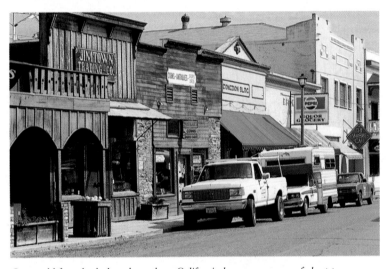

Once gold fever had abated, northern California became an area of ghost towns.

Fortunes and ghost towns

With gold selling at $15 an ounce, fortune-seekers made a profit of about $150 million in the four years between 1848 and 1852.

The Empire Mine, which went into production in 1850 and which was still being worked in 1956, yielded over 165 tonnes of gold.

1852 onwards, however, gold became harder to find, although the influx of gold-diggers continued unabated. New shafts were sunk right into the heart of mountains but by 1854, the main seams had been exhausted and the makeshift settlements that had sprung up around prospectors' camps became deserted. Soon, all that remained of the Gold Rush was the legend.

In the 1850s, an essential piece of kit for any well-equipped gold-digger was a Colt pistol, the only means of keeping unscrupulous neighbours at bay.

Yosemite Chapel is all that remains of a wooden village that was built in Yosemite Valley in the 19th century.

The snow-covered slopes of the High Sierra are thickly forested.

The great outdoors

As they explored the vast landscape of the American West or crossed the continent, pioneers and settlers alike could not fail to be impressed by the breathtaking beauty of the natural environment. Reacting against the great mining projects that were disfiguring the landscape, naturalists like John Muir spoke up for preserving the countryside. Their words were well received and, in 1864, Abraham Lincoln issued a decree to protect Yosemite 'for the use and enjoyment of all', making it the United States' first national park.

Whilst animals living in the national forests and parks of the Sierra Nevada are protected, elsewhere, efforts to save endangered species often clash with economic activities such as mining and logging.

The majestic landscape of Yosemite has inspired poets and adventurers alike.

Yosemite National Park

The Half Dome is one of the most extraordinary rock formations in the world and one of the strangest freaks of nature. This enormous outcrop of granite has been sliced in two by erosion and represents a major challenge for rock climbers.

Yosemite National Park, in the heart of the High Sierra, is famous not only for its spectacular scenery but also for its vegetation and wildlife, which vary according to altitude. This is a land of high peaks and ancient forest inhabited by bear and deer. The thick carpet of snow that covers the park in winter gives way to a profusion of flowers in spring and spectacular effects of light in autumn.

At Yosemite Creek, water tumbles over the precipice to land with a deafening roar some 2400 feet (740 metres) below.

For several months in winter, the Sierra Nevada once presented an impenetrable barrier to pioneers on their journey westward.

California's national parks, patrolled by park rangers, are open to one and all.

Other great national parks

Other national forests and parks lie within the Sierra Nevada on the eastern side of California. Here the topography, vegetation and wildlife epitomize the rugged beauty of the great American West. The majestic Kings Canyon, to the south of the High Sierra, is the lesser known rival of Colorado's Grand Canyon and is just one aspect of this dramatic landscape. From the heights of Mount Whitney, which rises to 14,491 feet (4418 metres), the canyon's vertical sides plunge to the depths of a chasm, making it the deepest in the United States.

Lassen Volcanic Park, away from the roads that run parallel to the Sacramento River as far as the north-western edge of California, is an area of rugged wilderness. Geysers and fumeroles are evidence of permanent volcanic activity.

The glacial waters of Lake Tahoe are over 1640 feet (500 metres) deep.

In summertime, Lake Tahoe is a highly popular holiday resort for Californians who come in search of fresh mountain air. For the physically active, mountain biking, paragliding and rock climbing are among the many activities that are on offer.

Lake Tahoe

Lake Tahoe, in the heart of the High Sierra, lies almost 6560 feet (2000 metres) above sea level. It is a place of unspoilt beauty and since the early 20th century has attracted many wealthy Californians. A world away from the bustle and commotion of towns and mines, Lake Tahoe is the idyllic location for many luxury summer residences. With the opening of casinos in the neighbouring

Squaw Valley: a centre for winter sports.

Surfing is a way of life in California, be it on the Internet, on the waves of the Pacific Ocean, or snowboarding in the High Sierra.

Donner Pass, near Lake Tahoe, was the scene of a tragedy during the winter of 1846–1847 when three families from Missouri became trapped there by a snowstorm. Some of their party went in search of help, but when rescuers finally arrived only 42 of the 89 people were still alive. In order to survive, these 42 had been forced to eat their fellow travellers.

state of Nevada in the 1930s, followed by the widely publicized Winter Olympics at Squaw Valley in 1960, the area became known to a wider audience. To exploit the commercial potential of the area's snow-covered slopes, some 20 ski resorts were built in the mountains around Lake Tahoe. The thick snow in these resorts holds the same excitement for skiing enthusiasts as the Pacific waves do for lovers of surfing.

The seeds of the sequoia germinate only in soil that has been cleared either by flooding or by a forest fire.

Sequoia National Park

Two species of sequoia grow in California. The giant sequoia grows at high altitudes on the western slopes of the Sierra Nevada whilst the coast or Californian redwood grows at lower altitudes around San Francisco. Their thick spongy bark enables them to survive forest fires.

In a secluded national park located on the western slopes of the Sierra Nevada grow sequoias, the largest of all living organisms. These trees, which can live for up to 4000 years, grow to majestic heights. The most famous example, known as 'General Sherman' stands over 275 feet (84 metres) high with a trunk that is 36 feet (11 metres) wide at the base – and it is still growing!

Sequoias have relatively shallow roots. Given this lack of anchorage, they are particularly vulnerable in strong winds.

Out towards Big Sur, Highway One passes through some spectacular scenery. Here the delicate outline of Bixby Creek Bridge blends into the intricately indented coastline.

Highway One is one of the most scenic routes in California, lined with vestiges of a Spanish heritage between San Francisco and LA.

The heritage of the missions.

Central Coast

Out towards the coast, the region is full of steep cliffs that receive the full pounding force of the Pacific Ocean as well as secluded creeks that are a haven for sea lions and colonies of sea birds. Further inland, there are Spanish missions and the holiday homes of rich Californians in search of unspoilt countryside. Central Coast seen from Highway One has inspired many artists and poets over the years. For the writer Henry Miller, this area was nothing less than heaven on earth.

After Mexican independence, the Spanish missions in California gradually became secularized and the new Mexican government redistributed the land that they owned.

By the beginning of the 17th century, much of the coast of California had been explored by Sebastián Vizcaíno, the Spanish navigator, who gave the names San Diego, Monterey and Santa Barbara to three of the natural harbours. It was not until 1769, however, that the area began to be settled. At that time, Spain put Father Junípero Serra in charge of setting up missions in what was then northern Mexico in order to bolster the sphere of

In California, the Spanish missionaries used building techniques that they had observed in Mexico. Adobe (sun-dried bricks made of earth mixed with straw) was the primary building material and the thick-walled buildings were then whitewashed with lime.

The 1920s saw a revival of interest in the architectural style of Spanish missions. The county court of Santa Barbara, built in 1929, is just one example.

Santa Barbara Mission, which was completely restored in 1953, is the only mission that has remained in Franciscan hands to this day.

The Spanish missions

The 21 missions that were established between San Diego and Sonoma from 1769 to 1833 were built in a mixture of styles that featured Romanesque, Moorish and Spanish elements. Most have been restored during the 20th century.

influence of a waning colonial power. As they made their way north, the Franciscan missionaries established some 20 missions along the Pacific Coast. On the pretext of converting the Native Americans, they seized their land and put them to work as agricultural labourers. At intervals of 10 leagues (about 30 miles / 50 km) they built a church, a fort (*presidio*) and a village (*pueblo*).

In the narrow creeks at the northern end of Central Coast, space is at a premium whenever large colonies of sea lions commandeer the beaches.

Monterey Bay

Monterey Bay was no exception to this extensive building programme. In 1604, Vizcaíno, discovered the anchorage and named it in honour of the viceroy of Mexico, the Count of Monte Rey. A century and a half later, Father Junípero Serra and the colonial governor Gaspar de Portola established the *presidio* of Monterey and the mission at Carmel, on the peninsula. The fort quickly became the political and military capital of California. It maintained this status right up until the Gold Rush, when it was superseded by Sacramento.

Highway One has a number of regular vantage points commanding panoramic views over the Pacific Ocean. Pods of whales can sometimes be seen in the distance.

Clint Eastwood: a Carmel cowboy

'America invented just two things: jazz and westerns.' This might be taken as a pejorative statement had it not been made by Clint Eastwood, a great jazz enthusiast and veteran of countless westerns. After studying at Oakland, Eastwood planned to go to Seattle University because of the jazz concerts that were put on there. Following a friend's suggestion, he took a screen test as a comedian; the experiment was successful and as a result, Universal Studios offered him his first contract. The many westerns in which he later starred made him one of the most famous names in Hollywood. He now lives quietly in Carmel where he was elected mayor for the term 1986–1988.

On the ranches of Central Coast, a stone's throw away from the untrammelled nature of the American West, horse-breeding is a serious business.

Monterey and Carmel

Throughout Central Coast, there are vestiges of the era of Spanish and Mexican domination. The region is dotted with lime-washed, red-roofed adobe houses and it is possible to imagine Zorro, the Wild West's answer to Robin Hood, galloping by on his black stallion with a posse of unscrupulous soldiers in hot pursuit. With the construction of the intercontinental railway at the end of the 19th century, however, this part of the Pacific Coast also began to attract tourists. As a result, a hotel complex was built. When it became known that Monterey Bay contained rich fishing

Works of art abound on Central Coast.

Polo and other exclusive sports reflect the standard of living on Central Coast, which is as high as anywhere in California.

In the coastal resorts between Santa Cruz to the north and Ventura to the south, the beaches are the focal point for a range of sports and other activities that have engendered a particular lifestyle. The cult of fitness and the body beautiful has since been exported throughout the world.

grounds, it then attracted Italian and Chinese fishermen, who, having long been whalers, now concentrated on fishing for sardines. Carmel, where the mission founded by Father Serra in 1770 has been completely restored, is now a quiet coastal resort. The mission itself is today still used as a Catholic church. Among the many people who now live in this little town is the actor and director Clint Eastwood.

The Fountain of Neptune at Hearst Castle is a reflection of the extravagant tastes of its owner, William Randolph Hearst, the Californian press baron.

The indoor pool is decorated with mosaics.

Throughout his life, William Randolph Hearst scoured the world for works of art with which to decorate the home that he regarded as being the epitome of rustic simplicity!

Orson Welles is said to have based the central character of his classic film Citizen Kane *(1941) on William Randolph Hearst.*

Hearst Castle is by far the most prominent building in the village of San Simeon. This luxurious pile fully reflects the megalomania of William Randolph Hearst, the man who had it built. Hearst, the multimillionaire and owner of the *San Francisco Examiner*, inherited a piece of land in the early 1920s. On it he had built his dream house: four buildings containing a total of over 150 rooms – all for him and his mistress!

Fabulously rich, and a powerful man who let nothing and no one stand in his way, he threw lavish parties in his Californian mansion which he shared with his mistress, the actress Marion Davies.

Organically-grown fruit and vegetables are all the rage on Central Coast.

Communing with nature...

A leisurely drive along Highway One reveals a world of fascinating natural beauty. This winding road follows the coastline where the terrain is often hilly. It is an area of unspoilt countryside, devoid of built-up areas between the beaches and the wooded coast. So impressive did the writer Henry Miller find this untouched landscape that he declared it to be 'heaven on earth'. Whether veiled in early morning mists, whipped by sudden squalls, lashed by heavy waves surging in from the Pacific, or bathed in strong afternoon sun, Central Coast is

The thermal springs in Ojai Valley have been known to Native Americans for centuries.

...on Highway One

unfailingly beautiful. Whilst Miller is no longer alive to enjoy this paradise, kindred spirits who take inspiration from such beauty can be found indulging in the simple pleasures of communing with nature. Those who embrace New Age philosophy find that this serenity is a stepping stone towards a deeper understanding of life. For others, the beaches are perfect for surfing.

The Californians of Central Coast have a special affinity with the Pacific Ocean which is never far away. Even in the pool halls of Central Coast, the surfboard is omnipresent.

In spite of its relaxed image, Santa Barbara is a rich and sophisticated resort.

Santa Barbara

Santa Barbara is one of the United States' top coastal resorts. Its permanently warm climate gives the impression that it is always summer – a place where the holiday season never ends.

Santa Barbara and its surroundings, on the border of Southern California, is the most southerly resort to retain the atmosphere particular to Central Coast. Almost completely destroyed by an earthquake in 1925, Santa Barbara was rebuilt largely in the architectural style of Spanish missions, a style which enjoyed a period of revival at the time. The houses are elegantly proportioned, with wide arches adorning their façades. This, combined with the resort's climate and fine sandy beaches, has made it the haunt of many artists and film stars.

Central Coast abounds with natural beauty. A river cascading into the Pacific Ocean is but one of the many breathtaking sights for which the coastline is famous.

Stretch limos symbolize the ostentatious wealth of the inhabitants of Beverly Hills, Los Angeles' richest residential district.

L os Angeles, the 'City of Angels', is the largest urban agglomeration in the United States. Its name conjures up images of great wealth, poverty... and Hollywood legends.

The sprawlng city of LA.

Los Angeles

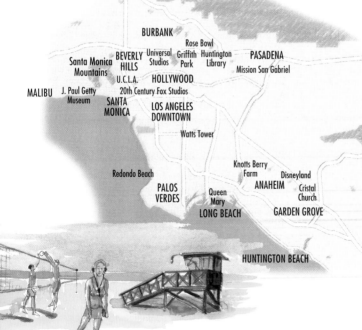

BURBANK

Rose Bowl

Beverly Universal Griffith Huntington   PASADENA
Santa Monica HILLS Studios Park Library   Mission San Gabriel
Mountains   U.C.L.A.   HOLLYWOOD

MALIBU   J. Paul Getty   20th Century Fox Studios
Museum   SANTA
MONICA   LOS ANGELES
DOWNTOWN

Watts Tower

Knotts Berry
Farm   Disneyland
Redondo Beach   ANAHEIM   Cristal
PALOS   Queen   Church
VERDES   Mary   GARDEN GROVE
LONG BEACH

HUNTINGTON BEACH

A basket of oranges against a background of skyscrapers and derricks. This was the image of Los Angeles in the 1930s.

In 1781, twelve Mexican families established a small *pueblo* (El Pueblo de Nuestra Señora la Reina de Los Angeles de Poricuncula) in what is now downtown Los Angeles. These villagers were soon joined by rancheros. The cattle that they raised provided hides for the New England shoemaking industry and, later, meat for the gold-diggers in northern California. In the saloons, whiskey flowed like water and

While the Yankee pioneers took possession of northern California by force and weight of numbers, their counterparts in southern California opted to convert to Catholicism and marry the daughters of wealthy Mexican ranchers. In the 1860s, however, a terrible draught brought ruin to the rancheros, who fell into debt and lost their lands.

In the 1920s, a forest of drilling platforms sprang up around the city.

Drilling for oil in the city

disagreements were settled with guns. With the completion of the transcontinental railway at the end of the 19th century, the town's population mushroomed. The installation of an aqueduct in 1913 that brought water all the way from the Sierra Nevada allowed Los Angeles to expand still further. During the same period, Edward Doheny sunk the first of the oil wells that were to make his fortune. The Los Angeles gold rush – this time for black gold – coincided with the burgeoning of the automobile industry.

In 1887, a price war between the two rail companies that served Los Angeles brought the price of a ticket from Chicago to Los Angeles down to $1. The majority of tourists who came to Los Angeles decided to stay.

Over one third of Los Angeles is covered by freeways, interchanges and parking lots. In downtown Los Angeles, this ratio rises to two thirds.

By the beginning of World War II, Los Angeles already had the highest ratio of cars to people in the world.

The cult of the car

In the wake of the oil boom and the automobile revolution, the population of Los Angeles increased dramatically and the city itself became a massive conurbation with endless suburbs. The car was now king and regulated daily life. Drive-ins sprang up everywhere, so that people could watch a movie, eat a hamburger or attend Mass, all without leaving the seats of their precious vehicles.

Over 1240 miles (2000 km) of railway tracks once served the various districts of Los Angeles but almost overnight the city's public transport system was abandoned in favour of roads. It was only in 1984 that the city started to run an underground railway system.

Colourful murals reflect the cultural heritage of immigrants from Mexico and, more recently, from all over Latin America.

The city without a centre

The Spanish-Mexican past of downtown Los Angeles lives on particularly strongly in El Pueblo, where shops sell traditional handicrafts and Mexican snack foods. El Pueblo is also the social centre of the city's Hispanic community.

As the 20th century progressed, the historic heart of the city lost its economic importance to newly developed districts and industrial zones lying on the outskirts. Efforts to breathe new life into this part of the city, with the installation of shopping centres, freeways and museums, failed to halt its decline, and the inner city areas, inhabited by Blacks and Hispanics, remain blighted by poverty.

In the neglected inner-city areas of Los Angeles, poverty, drug trafficking and racism are often rife.

In the 1980s, foreign investors bought up large areas of Los Angeles, owning up to 90 per cent of downtown properties.

The arrival of large Japanese companies has done much to revitalize the business district of Los Angeles.

Downtown

It is largely foreign capital that has been responsible for the development of Los Angeles over the past 20 years. Major banks have set up their headquarters in the high-rise office buildings around Flower Street. The Museum of Contemporary Art (MOCA), the Music Center, a huge public library and smart shops lure Angelinos and tourists to the formerly deserted city centre. These huge complexes now dwarf more classically inspired buildings such as the Bradbury Building (1893), whose Victorian decor was used as a backdrop to Ridley Scott's film *Blade Runner*.

Sunset Boulevard, made universally famous by the film of the same name, runs for 26 miles (42 kilometres) between downtown LA and the Pacific Coast Highway. The liveliest section is Sunset Strip, a focal point of Los Angeles nightlife.

'Low riding', cruising in a car (preferably a vintage model) with low suspension, is a favourite occupation among young chicanos (Americans of Hispanic extraction).

LA's criminal gangs

A simple freeway separates Downtown from the areas of Watts, LA's Black quarter, and Boyle Heights, the Hispanic district. Here, neat houses with well-kept lawns give the impression of peaceful, well-ordered lives. Appearances, however, can be deceptive. Boyle Heights, like Watts, is divided into zones controlled by rival gangs – the Rocks, the Evergreens and the Maravillas. Shoot-outs and undercover cocaine and crack dealing have earned these gangs a fearsome reputation, as portrayed in Dennis Hopper's film *Colors* (1988).

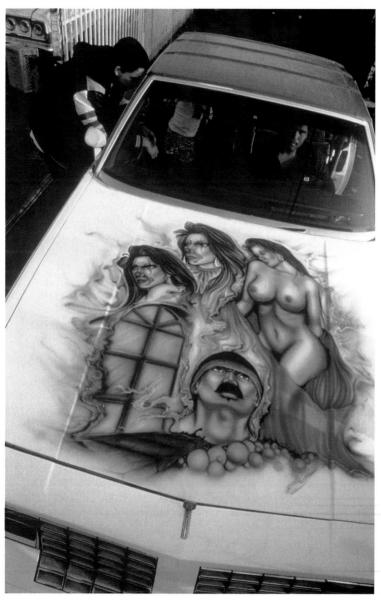

Young Angelinos were the first victims of drug trafficking in LA, which led to a culture of gun violence and gang warfare in poor inner-city areas.

Humphrey Bogart and Lauren Bacall in The Big Sleep *(1946), in which a detective tracks down dead bodies hidden in the Los Angeles home of an oil magnate.*

From the detective novel...

Made famous by such films as LA Confidential, *based on the novel by James Ellroy, the Los Angeles Police Department has a far from angelic reputation. Novelists and directors often portray the force as being riddled with corruption and racism at its most bigoted.*

Sam Spade, with his trilby pushed back on his head, feet up on the desk and bottle of bourbon at his elbow, is the epitome of the American detective as portrayed in novels and films. The character was created in the 1920s by the writer Dashiell Hammett. His successors were Philip Marlowe, Raymond Chandler's antihero, and Lew Archer, Ross Macdonald's intuitive detective. As California

Marilyn Monroe, more than any other screen goddess, epitomizes the cult of the Hollywood film star.

20ᵗʰ CENTURY FOX

...to the American cinema

invented the detective novel, so Hollywood launched the detective film. In 1941, Humphrey Bogart was offered the lead role in the film adaptation of Hammett's *The Maltese Falcon*. Even though the women playing opposite Bogey, Paul Newman or Robert Mitchum did not always have glamorous roles in these films, there was no shortage of actresses waiting in the wings. Mae West, Rita Hayworth, Ava Gardner and, of course, Marilyn Monroe head a long list of female stars who went on to become Hollywood legends, famous all over the world.

Marilyn

Marilyn Monroe, born Norma Jean Baker in Los Angeles in 1926, married for the first time at the age of 16. With the ambition of becoming a Hollywood star, she became a photographer's model in 1946 and had her first film successes in the early 1950s with *The Asphalt Jungle* and *All About Eve*. Her performances in *Some Like It Hot* and *The Seven Year Itch* established her career. A second marriage, to Joe DiMaggio, the greatest baseball player of his time, a third to Arthur Miller, the most celebrated playwright of the 1950s, a liaison with John F. Kennedy, president of the United States and a mysterious death following an overdose make up a legend with which the newspapers and the public at large continue to be fascinated.

Hollywood is often believed to form part of Los Angeles. It is, in fact, an independent district, even though it is completely surrounded by its powerful neighbour.

The golden age...

To have a star dedicated to you in the Walk of Fame, on the sidewalks of Hollywood Boulevard or Vine Street, is the ultimate accolade for any actor. Only 2500 have so far reached these heights of recognition.

At the start of the 20th century, New York was the centre of the American film industry. One or two producers seeking to work independently decided to move to Hollywood. The mild climate and almost permanent sunshine allowed them to make films in the open air virtually all year round. Soon, Hollywood became the place to be. While trench warfare raged in Europe, American cinema

Hollywood legends have made American cinema the world leader.

... of Hollywood

was conquering the world: 841 films were made in 1918 alone! Comedies staring Charlie Chaplin and Buster Keaton were huge box-office successes. Actors and directors such as Greta Garbo, Max Linder, Josef von Sternberg and Ernst Lubitsch began arriving from Europe. This was the golden age of Hollywood. Eight studios including Paramount, Warner, Columbia, Universal and United Artists, ruled Hollywood and shot 14,300 miles (23,000 kilometres) of film every year. Before long, contracts began binding film stars to certain studios.

Many famous stars have left their handprints or footprints in the concrete outside Mann's Chinese Theater (below). This tradition was started when a silent-film actress accidentally trod on the wet concrete.

Paramount Pictures was among the first of the major film studios to arrive in Hollywood. Ambitious young actors still come here in search of fame and fortune.

Beverly Hills

The Oscar, the film industry's most glittering prize, has been awarded by the Academy of Motion Picture Arts and Sciences since 1929. Although it is the most famous and most coveted prize, it is sometimes awarded for commercial success rather than excellence.

All the great Hollywood stars, from Bette Davis and Marlene Dietrich to Gary Cooper and Cary Grant, had houses built in Beverly Hills and were regularly seen in the bars and clubs along Sunset Strip. In 1939, *Gone with the Wind* heralded Hollywood's finest hour. With the outbreak of war, Fritz Lang, Alfred Hitchcock, and Jean Renoir left their native countries for Hollywood.

Beverly Hills' famous Marlboro man defiantly continues to light up despite widespread anti-smoking campaigns.

The Beverly Hills Hotel, built in the style of a Spanish mission, once welcomed the likes of Marilyn Monroe, Clark Gable, Richard Burton and Elizabeth Taylor.

Rodeo Drive in Beverly Hills has some of the most expensive shops in the world. Here, the well-heeled can buy jewellery or clothes by top French and Italian designers.

Like the Beverly Hills police, the local firefighters feature in many films and TV series.

Beverly Hills, the exclusive residential community favoured by stars of film and television, has become synonymous with wealth and glamour. Countless souvenirs enable tourists to buy a part of this dream.

The end of a legend

After World War II, antitrust laws and competition from the European film industry took their toll on Hollywood, in spite of new talent. At the beginning of the 1960s, television began to rival the cinema and the masterpiece of the decade, *2001: A Space Odyssey* was shot in London. Hollywood would have to wait for Steven Spielberg to match the box-office successes of the past.

Luxury residences nestle in thick vegetation that hides them from prying eyes and blocks out unsightly high-rise buildings.

From the hills to the bay

Beverly Hills, consisting of some 6 miles² (15 km²) of ostentatious luxury, today preserves no trace of the abandoned oil wells that could still be seen there at the beginning of the 20th century. In the hierarchy of sought-after addresses, however, Beverly Hills must bow to its even richer and more glamourous neighbour, Bel Air. This too is another world, inhabited by some of the country's biggest stars.

The beautiful gardens of private residences.

To the north-west of these residential areas lies Santa Monica Bay, a playground on the Pacific for the rich and famous of Los Angeles. Many celebrities have had second homes built along a stretch of the bay, so that access to the fine sandy beach is barred to the general public. Those out for a stroll can always head for Palisades Park, shaded by palm trees, from where the museum funded by John Paul Getty can be seen in the distance.

The gardens of the Getty residence were once home to the modern art collections now exhibited in the Getty Center. The multimillionaire had his home built in the style of a Roman villa, similar to those found in and around Herculaneum before the eruption of Vesuvius in 79 AD, decorating it with mosaics, paintings, fountains and statues.

Real life in Malibu is larger than fiction. The lifeguards on Malibu beach cultivate a look that has spread throughout the world thanks to TV series such as Baywatch.

The Los Angeles coastline, which runs from Malibu in the north to Laguna Beach in the south, has some of the finest beaches in the world.

A souvenir from LA.

The beaches of LA

All along the Los Angeles coastline, sun, sea, sky and endless golden beaches combine to produce a culture and way of life that are particular to California. Names such as Malibu, Santa Monica, Venice, Redondo, Long Beach and Huntington all conjure up images of life on the Pacific coast. For some, they will be associated with the cult of sunbathing and the body beautiful; for others surfing. As the settings of television soaps, these resorts have become familiar to millions all around the world.

Many cafés, restaurants and amusement parks fill the promenades, offering a welcome break from the sun and the beach.

The beaches of Los Angeles are instantly recognizable thanks to the power of television. To the north of Los Angeles lies Malibu Beach where the houses of film stars are built right on the sand and where there is some of the best surfing in

On the beaches of Los Angeles, even the police are 'cool'. Suntanned officers patrol on mountain bikes or even rollerblades!

the world. South of Malibu, towards Santa Monica, are the most exciting of the West Coast resorts, where a succession of beaches have everything the holidaymaker could ask for.

Venice Beach has a worldwide reputation for its bodybuilding gyms. In a land where 'big is beautiful', pumping iron is taken to the extreme.

The beaches of Los Angeles are an arena for free expression. Every kind of lifestyle, no matter how offbeat, is tolerated and goes unremarked.

On the West Coast, surfing has become a way of life. It is surrounded by a whole ethic that affects everything from clothes and colours to social conventions. For all that they may travel the world, the surfing fraternity always return to the beaches of Los Angeles.

The long surfboard is de rigueur.

Below Marina del Rey, which can justifiably claim to be the most important marina on the West Coast, lie the beaches that stretch to the south of Los Angeles' international airport. Of these, Redondo Beach is the most popular with surfing enthusiasts since the waves are considered to be the most even and regular in the world, after Hawaii. It is also from Redondo Beach that surfing was launched in the United

Although surfing was launched on the world from Redondo Beach, the major annual surfing competitions take place on Huntington Beach, south of Los Angeles.

Surfing on Redondo Beach

States. In 1907, George Freeth, fresh from Honolulu, demonstrated a completely new sport that immediately seized the imagination of young Angelinos. Lying flat on a long wooden board, Freeth propelled himself out to sea, turned, then slowly rose to his feet, cruising swiftly towards

George Freeth taught the first Californian surfers the finer points of the sport. His pupils included several well-known people, including the writer Jack London, who developed a passion for the new sport.

the shore on the crest of a strong wave. Before long, this new craze was sweeping the country.

On the West Coast, surfing has its a dry-land counterpart; rollerbladers 'surf' the streets, even in downtown Los Angeles.

In Los Angeles, even the most unexpected places can be transformed into skateboarding parks. This disused swimming pool is perfect.

You are what you eat. For those buying into the Californian lifestyle, a healthy diet is as equally important as exercise.

Beach culture

Whilst out on the Pacific, the water has been taken over by surfers, the beaches of Los Angeles have been turned over to the cult of the body beautiful. Body-building, weight-lifting, massage and suntan oil form a heady mixture of sights and smells. With everyone skateboarding or rollerblading, there is as much activity on the pavements and roads as there is on the ocean.

The Queen Mary *has been converted into a hotel off Long Beach.*

Long Beach...

Pasadena's Rose Bowl is the venue for the final of the American football college teams championship. This is a major event that is followed with interest throughout the United States.

Long Beach, with its large port, is a major industrial centre with key activities in the aerospace and petrochemical industries. The port stretches along the coastline of San Pedro Bay, where the Los Angeles River flows into the Pacific. Long Beach is, however, not just an industrial town with a busy port attached; the whole of the coastline, from Huntington Beach and Newport Beach all the way to Laguna Beach has been taken over by surfers. In Long Beach harbour, the *Queen Mary*, purchased in 1967 for $3 million, is now one of the area's more unusual hotels.

Disneyland makes the most of new technology.

...and attractions around LA

Los Angeles is surrounded by a host of other attractions. At Anaheim, for example, Walt Disney opened the doors to the first Disneyland in 1955, followed shortly afterwards by Knott's Berry Farm, a Wild West theme park. Pasadena, to the north-east of Los Angeles, is a centre for both sport and culture.

Crystal Cathedral was founded by the televangelist Robert Schuller. Visitors are struck by its grandiose proportions and by the evident religious fervour that pervades it.

It is home to many museums as well as the Rose Bowl, an arena used to stage American football.

The residential districts of San Diego, with their palm trees and blue skies, seem to epitomize the image of the American Dream.

I t was not until the fever of the Gold Rush and the quest for oil had abated that San Diego, a city bathed by the sun and the sea, came into its own.

San Diego's Spanish heritage.

San Diego

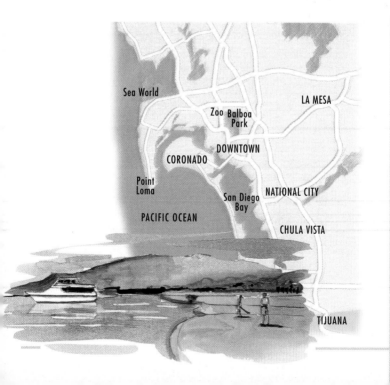

The marines of the US Navy form a significant proportion of the population of San Diego, making it the sixth most populated city in the United States.

In downtown San Diego, Balboa Park, named after Vasco Núñez de Balboa, the Spanish conquistador who discovered the Pacific Ocean, is an area of almost 1235 acres (500 ha) of greenery. Many of the pavilions for the 1915 Panama-Pacific World Fair were built in the park and have since been converted into museums.

A round of golf in front of the Yacht Club.

San Diego became a worthy rival of San Francisco and Los Angeles when the federal government decided to exploit the major strategic importance of its natural harbour. As the headquarters of the US Navy's Pacific fleet, San Diego is the largest military air force and naval base in the world. The presence of these air and naval bases has inevitably geared the city's economy to the development of the aerospace and electronic industries.

Decommissioned ships of the US Navy's Pacific fleet, leviathans of military might, are open to the public near San Diego Naval Station.

At San Diego's Sea World, whales and dolphins are trained to perform an impressive range of acrobatics, to the delight of their audiences.

The origins of San Diego's famous zoo go back to the 1915 Panama-Pacific World Fair.

Sea World and San Diego Zoo

The United States' first Sea World, where visitors can observe marine plants and animals at close quarters, was opened in San Diego in 1964. A major attraction are the performing seals, sea lions, dolphins and various species of whale, but Sea World also plays an important role in educating the public through programmes for the preservation of endangered species.

San Diego is a city of animal-lovers. The preservation of endangered species is a cause that the city enthusiastically supports.

'Eco-tourism' has created many jobs in San Diego, one of America's most important centres for the preservation of wildlife.

Murals in San Diego evoke the city's Spanish past and Native American roots.

San Diego's

Latin American influence is to be seen everywhere in San Diego. The murals that adorn the walls of the modern residential districts recall the adobe houses in the historic city centre. Present throughout California, this strong Hispanic flavour is not of course exclusive to San Diego; nevertheless, San Diego was the first mission to be founded in the 18th century by Spaniards as they gradually took possession of *Alta California* (Upper California). A garrison was then established there and a colony settled on the banks of the San Diego

Something of the flavour of San Diego's Mexican past lingers in Old Town, where the focal point is the Plaza. Even so, San Diego is very much an American rather than a Mexican city.

Hispanic heritage

River, a few miles from the bay. Located on the only overland route for expeditions on their way to settle the north, this newly established Spanish colony prospered through good times and bad, periodically fighting off attacks from Native Americans. Up until the 19th century, this was Mexican territory and Mexican culture took hold, spreading throughout the region. When Alta California became part of the United States, this deep-rooted Mexican culture persisted and although English took over as the spoken language, place names remained in Spanish.

A short history of California

Originally settled by the Spaniards, California at first formed part of Spain's Mexican empire. In 1821, after several popular uprisings, Mexico won independence. At that time, California, Texas and New Mexico, north of the Rio Grande, formed part of this newly independent country. A protracted period of great political instability then began; the old Spanish settlers and pioneers of Anglo-Saxon descent that made up the population of California felt ill at ease under Mexican rule. In 1845, Texas declared its allegiance to the United States which led to the Mexican War. The inhabitants of California then proclaimed their independence in 1848 and in 1850 California was admitted to the Union as the 31st state.

In San Diego, guards patrol the border on the lookout for illegal immigrants.

Tijuana and the border

The areas either side of the border between the United States and Mexico, at Tijuana, belong to two completely different worlds. Differences in the quality of life north and south of the border often lead to strained relations between the 'haves' and the 'have-nots'.

San Diego is located directly on the border between the United States and Mexico and has as its southern counterpart the Mexican city of Tijuana. For those north of the border, a trip to Tijuana means taking advantage of cheap Mexican goods. For those south of it, crossing over to San Diego is to step into the American Dream, even though that dream soon fades at the immigration desk.

Tijuana has always been a permissive playground for rich Americans. With a pocket full of dollars, gringos can behave in a way that would not be tolerated in San Diego.

At Zabriskie Point, in Death Valley, the Californian desert looks more like a lunar landscape than something of this world.

The area of land that lies between the US-Mexican border and the Sierra Nevada contains some of the most arid deserts in the world.

The motel: a modern oasis.

The southern deserts

The hot dry deserts that lie east of the climatic barrier formed by the Santa Rosa Mountains appear to be too hostile to support any form of life. Groups of nomadic Native Americans, however, managed to survive there by exploiting the deserts' scant resources. Later, determined efforts were made to extract deposits of borax from this arid landscape. Since then, human activity in Death Valley has been restricted mostly to arms testing and the tourist industry, which centres on Palm Springs.

Gigantic sand dunes give the Californian desert a mountainous landscape.

Southern California, baked by the scorching sun and subject to long periods of severe draught, stands in complete contrast to northern California and the Californian coast, where the climate is moderated by the Pacific Ocean.

Since 1886, when the first hotel was built in Palm Springs on the site of a thermal spring, the number of buildings has multiplied, transforming the small resort into a major tourist centre.

At the intersection between the Sonora Desert and the Mohave Desert, which stretches northwards to Death Valley, lies Palm Springs, a surprisingly verdant oasis in the middle of this arid region. Thanks

The arid Californian desert forms the backdrop to the golf courses of Palm Springs.

An unexpected oasis

to the exploitation of springs deep under the ground, water is in abundant supply. Paradoxically, this mid-desert resort has become the world capital of golf, with more than 80 lush golf courses. With its well-kept lawns, artificial lakes, carpets of flowers and thousands of palm trees covering hundreds of acres, Palm Springs rises like a permanent mirage from the surrounding arid hills and valleys. The San Bernardino Mountains provide welcome respite from the heat of the summer months, and have a number of good ski slopes in winter.

In Palm Springs, no self-respecting hotel would be without a swimming pool. Here, in the middle of a desert, the town boasts around 10,000 private swimming pools.

The Joshua tree can live for a thousand years and reach a height of 33 feet (10 metres).

Joshua Tree National Park

The deserts of California constitute an extraordinarily varied landscape, ranging from the great level expanses of dried lakebeds to the more mountainous terrain of the American West.

Joshua Tree National Park, which covers more than 741,300 acres (300,000 hectares) to the east of Palm Springs, contains many of the fleshy plants and curious rock formations that are common to the Low and Mohave Deserts. It is also home to the Joshua tree, a rare species of yucca that was given its name by Mormon pioneers, and to a number of animals that are surprisingly well adapted to life in this inhospitable environment. Among them are coyotes and the fleet-footed roadrunners on which they prey. To cross this region is to

Small towns are welcome oases along the roads that cross the Californian deserts.

Truckers who drive across the deserts of California have about them something of the pioneers who, in their heavy covered wagons, made their way across the vast continent to the West Coast.

embark on a voyage of discovery. The only sparse signs of civilization, past or present, are a few solitary towns, one or two old abandoned mines and a handful of wayside resting places where time seems to have stood still. In this land of dust clouds and majestic landscapes, the sun beats down mercilessly on cars and trucks as they speed along straight roads and disappear into the shimmering horizon.

These desolate landscapes contrast sharply with the packed beaches of Central Coast.

The Mohave Desert

Adventures set in barren landscape are the stuff of legend that perpetuate a popular vision of the American West that lives on to this day. Travelling northwards, you soon come across the trail taken by the pioneers and prospectors on their way from Santa Fe to the Pacific coast. Here, the landscape becomes even more desolate as the route leads into the Mohave Desert, home to

Huge areas of the Mohave Desert are closed to the public. They are used by the US Army for training and for testing its latest weapons. Many of these army exercises are carried out using live ammunition.

Like many of the arid regions in California, Death Valley, surely one of the most inhospitable places on earth, consists of some extraordinarily varied landscapes.

Red Rock Canyon, an untamed wilderness.

the dreaded Death Valley. Inhabited by rattlesnakes and devoid of drinkable water, this isolated location is the perfect choice of site for the US Air Force's main secret weapons-testing base. Since 1933, test pilots have assured American military prowess in the air. It was here, in a desert that regularly rumbles to the sound of test flights and the landing of the space shuttle, that Chuck Yeager first broke the sound barrier.

Some 490 feet (150 m) deep and 2625 feet (800 m) wide, the Ubehebe Crater was formed about 4000 years ago. It's gigantic proportions are perfectly in keeping with the massive scale of the American West.

The dunes of Stovepipe Wells cover 15 miles^2 (40 km^2) in the heart of Death Valley.

Death Valley...

In the 1920s, Albert Johnson, a multimillionaire with a fascination for the desert, teamed up with 'Death Valley Scotty', an adventurer who had taken part in Buffalo Bill's Wild West Show, and spent $2 million building a ranch in Death Valley, known as Scotty's Castle.

Red Rock Canyon, not far from Death Valley, presents yet another face of the Mohave Desert: its many fabulous rock formations have made it an ideal location for shooting science fiction films. A few abandoned mines here and there are the only remaining traces of those brave or foolhardy prospectors who, in the late the 19th century, tried their luck without much success. Death

Zabriskie Point is one of Death Valley's most famous features.

...the gaping jaws of hell

Valley, whose lowest point is 269 feet (82 m) below sea level, is where the highest temperatures in North America have been recorded. It is a place where the only vestiges of life are bones bleached by the sun and salt that covers the ground. Some 140 miles (225 kilometres) long, Death Valley fully deserves its name; those rare pioneers who took it upon themselves to cross this furnace set themselves a task of Herculean proportions. To Native Americans, Death Valley was known as *Tomesha*, 'the land where the ground is on fire.'

The spot known as Dante's View offers a glimpse of an inferno such as the Italian poet might have imagined.
In Death Valley, 'only the stones are alive', according to an ancient Native American saying.

Creative Workshop

*Having discovered the wonders of California,
it's now time to get creative.*

*All you need are a few odds and ends and a little
ingenuity to keep the spirit of your adventure alive
by creating your own beautiful craft objects.*

*These simple yet ingenious ideas capture the special
flavour of California and leave you with a permanent
reminder of your visit.*

*An original, simple and fun way to preserve
your holiday memories.*

Silicon Valley Picture Frame

*T*his picture frame will make the perfect surround for the craziest snapshots of your Californian holiday. This state-of-the-art frame looks as though it might have been dreamed up by one of the computer boffins of Silicon Valley.

Making the frame

• Remove the glass from a clip frame. Place it on the polystyrene and trace the outline.

• Remove the centre of the polystyrene by cutting out a rectangle 1/4" (5 mm) inside this outline. Trim the outer edges of the polystyrene at an angle so as to create an uneven rectangle.

• Save a few offcuts to use as wedges for securing the glass. Use the rest to stick on the front of the frame.

• Cut strips out of newspaper and completely cover the frame with them, fixing them in place with glue.

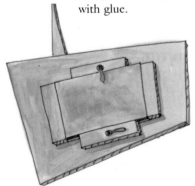

Colouring the frame

• When the glue has dried, apply a first coat of green paint. Roughly mix some white paint with the green and apply a second coat to produce a marbling effect.

Adding the Silicon Valley touch

• Decorate the frame with parts of transmitters and lengths of copper wire. Use the superglue to fix them in place.

Fixing the glass

• Secure the glass behind the polystyrene. Stick four strips of polystyrene around the edges of the glass as shown on p 132.

• Lay your photograph face down on the glass and place the backing card from the clip frame on top of it.

• To keep the glass in place, use the rectangle of polystyrene that you cut out of the centre and place it over the backing card.

• To secure the polystyrene, screw two small clips to the polystyrene strips at the back of the frame (as shown on p 132).

Adding the stand

• To make a stand for the frame, fix a small bracket to the back. Alternatively, add a hook to hang it from the wall.

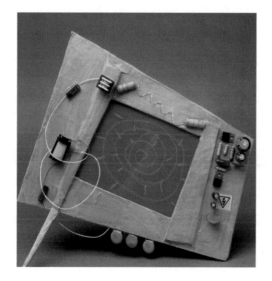

Materials

• a sheet of polystyrene about 8" x 12" (21 cm x 30 cm) • newspaper • paper glue • superglue • a tube of green acrylic paint • a tube of white acrylic paint • two small plastic picture frame clips • a piece of glass or transparent plastic, such as found in a clip frame, about 4" x 6" (10.5 cm x 15 cm) • parts of transmitters (such as found in old radios) • a Stanley knife • a paintbrush

Hollywood Paving Stone

*M*ake your own Hollywood paving stone like the ones found outside Mann's Chinese Theater. Press your hands into wet concrete, add your name and hey presto...a new star is born!

Making the frame

• Nail the four pieces of wood together at right angles to make a square mould. Cover the wooden board with the bin liner, making sure that it is nice and flat.
• Place the wooden mould on top and secure it with a few nails inserted round the outside edge.
• Thoroughly oil the inside wooden surfaces that will come into contact with the cement.

Adding the cement

• In a bucket, mix the quick-drying cement with a little water following the manufacturer's instructions.
• Pour the liquid cement into the wooden casing and smooth it over with the trowel.

Making your mark

• When the cement has begun to set (after about half an hour, although the time will vary according to the type of cement you use), smear your hands with oil or hand cream so as to protect your skin.

• Press your hands, palm down, into the cement, pushing hard for a few seconds so as to leave quite a deep print. Write your name and the date in the concrete with the end of a pencil.

• The edge of the concrete slab

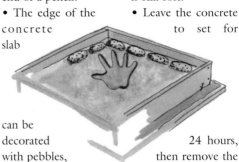

can be decorated with pebbles, pressing them into the concrete while it is still soft.

• Leave the concrete to set for 24 hours, then remove the wooden casing.

Materials

• 4 lengths of wood 1 1/2" x 1/2" x 16" (4 cm x 1.5 cm x 40 cm) • 20 nails
• a wooden board 20" (50 cm) square • a bin liner • 15 lb (7 kg) of quick-drying cement • oil • an old bucket • a trowel • a pencil • pebbles (optional)

Victorian Details

San Francisco's Victorian houses are renowned
for their façades, which are adorned with a variety
of decorative details. By making replicas of some of
these details, you can add a touch of authentic San
Franciscan elegance to the furniture in your own home.

Preparing the design

• Enlarge the motif (shown left) on a photocopier and fix it to the plywood with spray mount or sticky tape. Alternatively, use a soft pencil to draw the enlarged motif on tracing paper and trace it onto the wood.

Cutting out

• With the two clamps, secure the plywood to the edge of a workbench. Take care that the saw will not damage the bench.
• First cut out the inner sections, then cut round the outer shape.

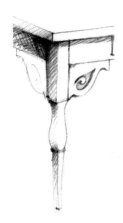

Sanding and painting

• Sand the pieces first with medium-weight sandpaper, then with fine-grained sandpaper. Round off all the edges expect those forming right angles.

• Apply two coats of paint. Leave to dry.

Assembling

• Spread wood glue to the straight outer edges of the pieces and fit them inside the right angles of a piece of furniture, such as under a shelf or at the top of a table leg. The pieces can also be secured using metal brackets.

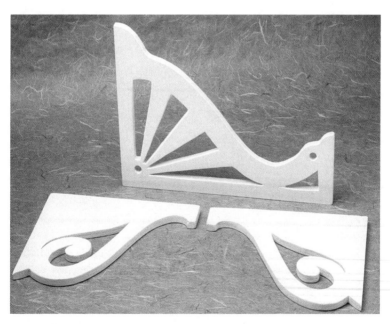

Materials

• plywood 1/3" (9 mm) thick • an electric fretsaw • a can of spray mount or sticky tape and tracing-paper • 2 joiner's clamps • medium and fine sandpaper
• satin-finish acrylic paint • a medium-fine paintbrush • metal brackets or wood glue

Gold Nugget Buttons

These gold-diggers' buttons make eye-catching accessories. Simply substitute the buttons of almost any waistcoat for these attractive gold nuggets, which can also be worn as a brooch on the collar of a coat, or as a necklace.

Making the nuggets

• Knead the clay then roll it into little balls just large enough to pass through the buttonholes of your waistcoat.

• Gently press each ball on an even surface so as to give it a flat back. With the tips of your fingers model the balls to give them an irregular shape, then prod them with the blunt end of a pencil to create the uneven surface of gold nuggets.

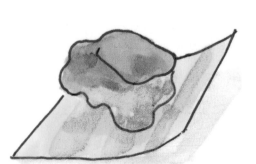

Applying the gold

• Roll each nugget in a separate piece of gold leaf and rub it so that it sticks to the clay.

• Bake for 20 minutes in an oven preheated

to Gas Mark 4 (120°C, 250°F). If you are not using gold leaf, bake the nuggets as they are then cover them with gold paint.

Attaching the buttons

Fix the pin part of the button attachment to the nugget with a drop of superglue.

• Now attach them to your waistcoat, arranging them in a vertical line down the front so that they pass through the button-holes. Add the clasp at the back to hold them in place.

• You can also wear the nuggets as brooches, perhaps arranged in a line on the collar of a jacket.

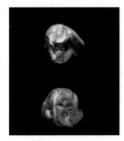

Materials

• brown Fimo polymer clay • two-part button attachments (consisting of a pin and a clasp)
• 1 piece of gold leaf for each button, or gold paint • superglue

Redcurrant Milkshake

*T*he taste of an all-American milkshake is guaranteed to bring back vivid memories of your trip to the West Coast of the United States. This thirst-quenching, refreshing and healthy drink can also be served as a dessert.

Making the flavoured milk

• Wash the redcurrants and carefully pick them off their stalks.

• Place them in a food mixer with the sugar and purée them.

• Add two glasses of milk to the purée to obtain a liquid mixture.

• Remove the pips by passing the mixture through a sieve.

Mixing the ingredients

• Beat the egg yolks together with the vanilla sugar. Then fold in the yoghurts and beat the mixture again.

• Pour this mixture into the food mixer.

• Add the flavoured milk and mix well.

• Gradually add the rest of the milk, switching on the mixer in short bursts so as to produce a thick creamy milkshake.

Serving

• Pour the milkshake into tall glasses and decorate each with a sprig of redcurrants as shown. Add a straw to each glass and serve immediately. In summer, the milkshake can be served chilled.

Ingredients

- To serve 8 people
- 1lb 2oz (500g) of redcurrants, reserving a few sprigs for decoration
- 3 1/2oz (100g) of caster sugar • 2 1/2 pints (1.5 litres) of fresh milk
- the yolks of two eggs • 4 sachets of vanilla sugar • 2 plain yoghurts

INDEX

Acknowledgements

The publishers would like to thank all those who have contributed
to the preparation of this book, in particular:

Guy-Claude Agboton, Angie Allison, Aude Desmortiers,
Rupert Hasterok, Nicolas Lemaire,
Hervé Levano, Marie-Bénédicte Majoral, Mike Mayor,
Kha Luan Pham, Marie-Laure Ungemuth

Creative Workshop:
Evelyne-Alice Bridier (p. 132-135), Valérie Zuber (p. 136-139)

Translation: Lucilla Watson

Illustrations: Franz Rey, Valérie Zuber

Printed in Italy
Eurolitho - Milan
March 1999